910.4
O'Gr

O'Grady, Philippe

Escape from the Island of Ice

	DATE DUE		
9-30			
10-6			
10-8			
11-6			
11-20			
11-30			
2-1			
SEP. 25			
28			
MAR. 4			

ESCAPE FROM THE ISLAND OF ICE

ESCAPE FROM THE ISLAND OF ICE

Philippe O'Grady

Illustrated by Scott Zoellick

RAINTREE PUBLISHERS
Milwaukee • Toronto • Melbourne • London

Library of Congress Number: 79-22723

1 2 3 4 5 6 7 8 9 0 84 83 82 81 80

Printed and bound in the United States of America.

Library of Congress Cataloging in Publication Data

O'Grady, Philippe.
 Escape from the island of ice.

 SUMMARY: Describes the 800-mile sea journey in a 20-foot boat made by Sir Ernest Shackleton and 5 other men in order to seek help for the stranded companions of their Antarctic expedition.

 1.   Antarctic regions — Juvenile literature.
[1.   Imperial Trans-Antarctic Expedition, 1914-1917.
2.   Shackleton, Sir Ernest Henry, 1874-1922.   3.   Antarctic regions.   4.   Survival]   I.   Zoellick, Scott.
II.   Title.
G863.O36   910'.45   79-22723
ISBN 0-8172-1562-X lib. bdg.

CONTENTS

CHAPTER 1

A Walk Across a Continent

Many famous names are connected with the time of the great South Pole explorations. Among them are the American admiral, Richard E. Byrd. And, of course, there was the Norwegian, Roald Amundsen. Amundsen was the first man to reach the South Pole. In all the history of Antarctica, however, no adventure matches that of Sir Ernest Shackleton and the crew of the explorer ship *Endurance*.

Shackleton's expedition across Antarctica was a mighty try, even though it failed. It taught the world what it means to be brave when faced with great danger—even death. Shackleton never gave up the fight. He believed in what he was doing, even when it became impossible to go on.

By not giving up and by putting others ahead of himself, Shackleton turned failure into success. He and his men overcame great odds. Even though they never reached their goal, their story

lives on. It has become an example to others.

––––––––

There was nothing in Ernest Shackleton's background to say that one day he would become a famous and honored explorer. He was born in Ireland in 1874. His family were well-to-do landowners and teachers. When he was still very young, Ireland faced a depression. It had been brought about by huge crop failures. Shackleton and his family moved to England. There his father, a doctor, set up a practice in the suburbs of London.

At school, Shackleton began reading adventure stories. One of his first heroes was Captain Nemo of Jules Verne's novel *20,000 Leagues Under the Sea*. He began thinking of a life spent in charting the unknown. He daydreamed constantly about going to sea someday.

When Shackleton's schooling was over, his cousin arranged for him to sign on as a member of the *Mercantile Marine*. At first, he was laughed and jeered at by the rest of the crew of more experienced seamen. He had packed a book of poetry along with the rest of his belongings.

When his apprenticeship ended, Shackleton decided that the sea was the only career for him. He signed on as mate aboard several other ships. It was at this time that he began hearing tales of the first polar expeditions. He heard that the Royal Geographical Society was planning to explore the vast and mysterious continent of Antarctica. And he longed to join in the adventure.

His first trip south was as a member of Captain Scott's party aboard the *Endeavor* in 1901. Captain Scott had great trust in young Shackleton. The captain felt he could count on the young man. The expedition managed to travel farther south than any group had up to that time. But they did not make it to the South Pole. Shackleton became ill, and Captain Scott ordered him to return to England. Shackleton was disappointed at not being able to complete the mission. But

this feeling only made him surer of what he would do. One day he would lead his own expedition.

At the beginning of 1907, Shackleton announced that he was going to make a series of trips to try and reach the South Pole himself. Since he was not able to get any government help, he had to depend upon private backing. He had gained fame as a leader on Captain Scott's expedition. Because of this, Shackleton had no trouble getting the finest, most experienced men to join him.

Troubles followed his ship from the very beginning. They faced snow, bad weather, and a shortage of food. Shackleton and his party did, however, come closer to the South Pole than Captain Scott had.

The early years of the 1900s were filled with tales of the exploration of the Antarctic. The newspapers and magazines of the day carried many stories about it. And the adventures of the brave explorers caught the imagination of the British people. In the 1950s and 1960s space exploration would affect the American people in the same way. School children dreamed of becoming explorers themselves, just as Shackleton had. Shackleton suddenly found that he was famous.

He was still unhappy, however. In 1912

Amundsen and his group had been the first to reach the South Pole. That part of the dream was over for Shackleton. But Shackleton felt that he must go on exploring. He believed that if he gave it up, people would think he had failed.

Shackleton decided, then, that he would change his plan. He could not be the first to reach the South Pole. But he could lead the first party to cross the frozen continent of Antarctica from coast to coast. His plan was to leave Buenos Aires aboard the *Endurance* and land his team on the Weddell Sea coast. There they would begin their long and dangerous trip. They would cross the uncharted land to the opposite end of the continent.

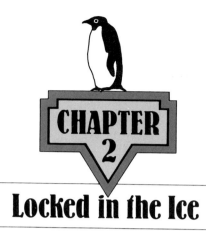

Locked in the Ice

In October 1914, the First World War began storming throughout Europe. At that same time, Ernest Shackleton arrived in the city of Buenos Aires, in Argentina. It was here that he planned to begin the first leg of his great journey. His dream was becoming a reality.

Shackleton had chosen Frank Worsley, a New Zealander, to be skipper of the tough, wooden-hulled Norwegian ship, the *Endurance*. The *Endurance* would carry them and their party to the Weddell Sea. The Weddell Sea branches off from the South Atlantic Ocean. Here they would sail to a point on the coast. From this point they would begin their trip across the frozen continent. Shackleton figured that the trip would not take longer than five months.

The *Endurance* was being made ready to set sail. A young British sailor named Blackboro begged to be taken along. His dream was to make this historic trip with the famous Shackleton. But Shackleton felt that the boy was too young and too green to face the hardships that lay ahead. He refused. It was only after several days at sea that they discovered the young sailor had stowed away. He had hidden himself in a chest where oilskins were kept. At first, Shackleton was angry. But he could understand Blackboro's longing and drive.

Shackleton convinced Captain Worsley to take on the young sailor. Blackboro was accepted on the crew. Later he became a steward.

Shackleton expected his men to do their work well. He would not stand for anything less. Everything had to be exactly right. Everything. He made a point of getting to know each member of

the crew. He also felt that a proper diet was just as important to the men as was keeping them happy. Early in the trip, he set a strict program that included fresh food and a high level of fitness. His stern face and his rules earned him the title "The Boss."

By November, the *Endurance* reached the whaling station at Grytriken on South Georgia, one of the Falkland Islands just above the Antarctic. Three days out of South Georgia, the ship met its first belt of heavy pack ice.

Pack ice is a sort of jigsaw puzzle of ice. Sometimes it drifts a little way apart. At other times, it

locks together so tightly that a ship cannot go on any farther. At first, the *Endurance* was able to ram its own way into open water. But it soon became jammed in the heavy ice.

They tried waiting for the ice to break up so that they could go on. After a time, Shackleton decided to take matters into his own hands. He ordered the crew to try to smash their way through the ice with chisels and special ice picks. But there was no way out of this frozen trap. Although they were only twenty-five miles from their goal, they couldn't move. The pack was freezing harder than ever around the ship. And Shackleton knew that they had come to a complete halt. He gave orders for the ship's routine to be made looser. The crew set about preparing to spend a winter on the ice.

The *Endurance* underwent a change from a seagoing vessel to an ice-locked winter station. Some of the dogs that had been brought along on the expedition had died at sea. Shackleton's men built shelters on the ice for the animals that remained. These dogs would later be very important to them.

Shackleton knew that one of the major problems to be faced was boredom. He kept spirits high by giving each man on the crew a certain task. He also made each of them feel that he was an important, needed part of the expedition. Shackleton entertained the men with talks about his earlier travels. They also passed the time by playing ice hockey and by holding Dog Derbies, in which the dogs would race each other along the ice.

By April, the entire pack that closed in the *Endurance* began floating south. It was not long before the ship began to heave and crack. This could mean only one thing. The long-awaited thaw had finally arrived!

But with the thaw came new problems. The ice was so thin in spots that it became dangerous to walk on it. Seal hunting was impossible. Because of the lost time, food was in very short supply. And so the men had to cut back their rations.

The constant pressure of the ice grinding against the ship soon became too much for it. Leaks began to spring up. The ship was no longer safe. It became clear to Shackleton that he had no choice. They would have to abandon ship and set up camp on the ice. Shackleton and his men shared one final dinner aboard the *Endurance*. Then they prepared to leave it to make a new home on the ice. Water was already swirling through the holds. They took the three lifeboats and what was left of the food stores.

The ice was slowly crushing the tough old ship

before his very eyes. Shackleton knew that the ship was doomed. He and his men would have to get to civilization by other means. His plan was to trek across the frozen sea to Paulet Island. There he knew that a Swedish exploring party had left a hut with supplies from their expedition nearly fifteen years earlier.

Five tents were pitched on the ice. Shackleton explained to his men that they were going to have to march to Paulet, dragging the lifeboats with them. That night they slept to the sound of the ice grinding about them.

The next morning they prepared for the long journey across the ice to shelter and safety.

CHAPTER 3

The Ship Sinks

Dragging their lifeboats behind them, the members of the group could travel only a total of about nine miles over a period of several days. They realized that they had set out on a hopeless task. From time to time, various members of the team would return to the *Endurance* to take off more supplies. They hunted all over the ship, trying to find whatever could be saved. By now the *Endurance* was slowly sinking beneath the icy waters.

Barrels of nuts, jams, and flour were found in the hold. These were brought back to the temporary shelter, which Shackleton named Ocean Camp. A box of photographs was also located. Since the box had been stored in a watertight tin, the photographs had not been spoiled. These pictures were later to become very valuable to historians and scholars. They recorded exactly the way the *Endurance* looked during every stage of its winter drift.

Ocean Camp was located on a large, thick ice floe that Shackleton judged to be about two years old. The older the floe, the more solid it is. A two-year-old floe would be able to stand the weight of the men and their gear without cracking.

One of the last trips back to the *Endurance* for supplies was a sad one for Shackleton and the men he had brought. They watched the gallant old ship, which had carried them so far away from their homes, sink slowly beneath the ice. With it also went Shackleton's hopes of a successful expedition. Now all of his thoughts centered on getting his men to civilization and safety.

At Ocean Camp, the members of the group waited for the ice to drift. The Boss still made his crew follow a fitness program. The men passed part of the daylight hours in exercising. The rest of their work included looking after the dogs and mending their tents.

The carpenter spent his time mending the three lifeboats. These boats could mean the difference between living and dying.

When their chores were over, they relaxed. They played cards, read, and sang songs. One of the men had found a banjo before the *Endurance* was abandoned.

Finally the ice was again firm enough for hunting parties to go out. They brought back plenty of seal meat. The food shortage was over. But as time passed, the ice began breaking up at a much faster rate. Shackleton had to set up a rigid watch patrol. All during the long Antarctic nights, they were on the lookout for cracks. Such cracks would mean that they had to leave their temporary home at Ocean Camp.

By December, the breakup had reached such a point that Shackleton knew that he and the men would be forced to move on again. It was several days before Christmas. Shackleton decided that they would celebrate the holiday on their last night at Ocean Camp. Everyone's spirits were lifted briefly. Then the long, slow trek over the ice began again.

They traveled only during daylight hours. At night they made camp. Tensions began to grow among the men. Even Captain Worlsey and the ship's carpenter broke into a fight at one point. The Boss was severe in his criticism of their behavior. He was trying to do his best to hold the party together. He knew that, in order to survive, they must all work together. Otherwise, all would be lost.

Shackleton directed the movement toward another old ice floe. There they once again pitched their tents. They named this site Patience Camp. They knew they would have a long wait there. And they would need to be patient.

The food problem ended when one of the men shot a huge, 1000-pound sea leopard. But food was not their only problem. The ice around the camp was wet and dangerous. The men had to stay in their tents. It was too risky to move about on the floe. The melting ice meant that it would be impossible to travel across it. Shackleton knew that all of their hopes to reach Paulet Island lay in the lifeboats.

Patience Camp slowly began to fall apart. The state of the ice made it impossible to go anywhere on foot. The floe was moving rapidly along with the rest of the pack. Shackleton knew that the moment had arrived for the boats to be put into the water.

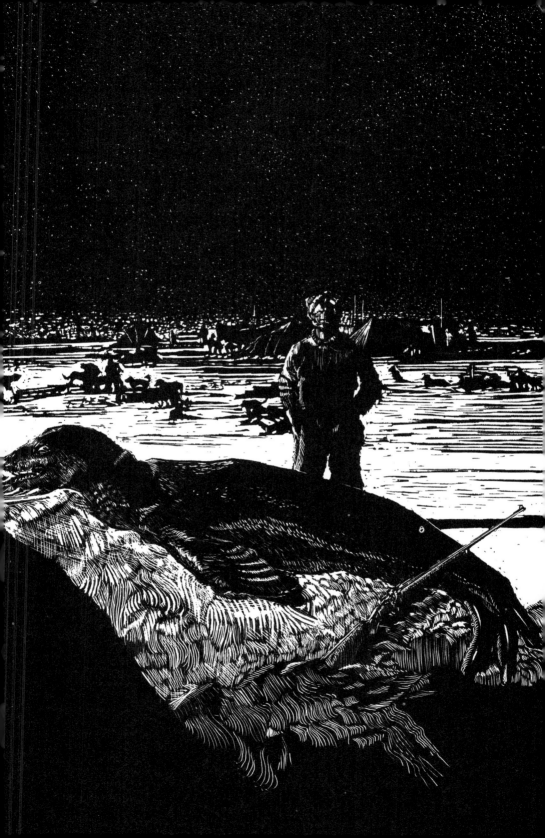

The members of the expedition manned the three boats and set off in them. After the first day on the water, Shackleton tried to set up camp on another floe. The melting ice nearly trapped them. And Shackleton swore they would stay away from all ice floes from that point on. They would remain in the boats.

It soon became clear that a strong current had carried the lifeboats badly off course. A new island destination was chosen. For the next several days, the three boats fought on through heavy weather and very rough seas.

Lying in the darkness of the lifeboats, the men tried to catch a few moments of much needed sleep. All around them were the sounds of the

terrible killer whales. The men knew that they would need all of their energy. Yet they could get no rest. All their hopes rested with The Boss. Shackleton knew that the entire party was depending on him. He prayed that they would soon sight land.

Finally a hungry, thirsty, and sick Shackleton found the answer to his prayers. Elephant Island came into sight. He had not let his men down.

Looking for a safe place to land, the three little boats started toward the dangerous and forbidding coast of the island. They had to move the boats about for a full day before they finally were able to put ashore on a tiny beach, 100 feet by 50 feet.

For the first time in 497 days, Shackleton and his party planted their feet on land. After getting their fill of water and sleep, the members of the expedition felt strong again. They killed a number of penguins and seals for food. For the time being, they were free of the hardships of the icy seas. And they celebrated their freedom.

CHAPTER 4

Five Set Out Alone

One of the lifeboats went on a scouting trip up the coast of the island. The men located what seemed to be a better beach. They returned to the other boats to tell the rest of the men of their find. And the three boats moved on.

On the way back to the second beach, they were caught in a heavy storm and nearly didn't make it. When they did, Shackleton realized that the new beach did not offer much more than the first. Their efforts had been in vain.

Conditions on the tiny island were harsh. Savage winds and snowstorms made day-to-day living very hard. Shackleton knew that Elephant Island, which was only twenty-three miles long and thirteen miles wide, was off the track of whaling and sealing boats. Their chances of being spotted by any passing ships were very small.

He decided that their only hope was to form a

party to take the sturdiest of the lifeboats and go back to the whaling station on South Georgia. They would then have to cross the dangerous Drake Passage. From there they could arrange for a relief ship to come back for the remaining members of the party.

He called for volunteers to make the perilous trip with him. By this time, the men's faith in The Boss was so great that every man in the group volunteered.

Finally, he chose the four strongest, healthiest men. They prepared the lifeboat, which had been named the *Caird* for one of the backers of the expedition. The *Caird* was a light craft and was twenty-two feet long. They borrowed the

mast from one of the other lifeboats to make the keel of the *Caird* stronger. Then they waited for the weather to clear so they could push off.

The storms let up. Shackleton, Captain Worsley, and the chosen volunteers prepared for their journey. During the launching, two of the men fell overboard. Then a rock drove a hole through the hull. They had to wait again until the carpenter had repaired it.

Finally, they took on supplies and set sail for South Georgia. Looking back toward Elephant Island, Shackleton saw the men he had had to leave behind on shore. He swore to himself that, at any cost, he would do his best to rescue them as soon as possible. He knew that time was impor-

tant. The men were weak. They couldn't hold out much longer.

The remaining crew members watched the *Caird* sail out of sight. Then they set about preparing a hut for shelter, using the two remaining lifeboats. They turned one upside down against a wall of rocks and began the long wait for Shackleton to get help.

Bad weather made their lives more and more miserable. Yet the men did their best to try and keep up each other's spirits. They knew The Boss would have done the same if he had been there with them.

The former stowaway, Blackboro, developed severe frostbite. He was saved from danger when one of his fellow crewmen amputated his toes.

As the long Antarctic winter went on and on, the men on Elephant Island never lost hope that Shackleton would return for them and take them to safety. It was all they had to go on.

Meanwhile, aboard the *Caird*, Shackleton was busy trying to create a feeling of security for the men he had brought with him. He still insisted on regular meals and a strict routine.

The ice began settling, making the *Caird*'s progress slower. The journey became more and more wearying. Because of the small amount of space, the men were very uncomfortable. To add to their other problems, their water supply was running dangerously low. Then a gale blew up, and made the sea so rough that they nearly turned over several times. The *Caird* was almost driven back to the ice pack.

The cold was intense. Shackleton was wet and thirsty and ill. Still he remained cheerful. He was more determined than ever to return to the pack and rescue his men.

At times the sea was so stormy that, in order to take a sighting to know where they were, Captain Worsley had to be held up on each side. Otherwise he could easily have fallen overboard.

When the bad weather let up a bit, Captain Worsley was able to figure out that they had made it one-third of the way to South Georgia Island. Going on, they were aided by heavy winds that blew them to the halfway point.

The small group faced more bad weather, thirst, hunger, and mental and physical exhaustion. Finally, however, they spotted South Georgia Island through the constant mist that blurred the sun.

But their problems were far from over. A heavy wind kept them from making a landing that day. The next morning, a hurricane blew up. As the *Caird* was carried toward the island, out of control, the men prayed that they would be able to find a safe landing before being smashed to pieces against the rocky cliffs.

They struggled for all they were worth. Finally, they made it to a tiny bay on the island's coast. There, they pulled into a small cove where they were able to step ashore.

Shackleton and his men found a small cave for shelter. They killed some baby albatross for food. They were so hungry that they devoured the birds, nearly eating the bones as well. Then they treated themselves to some melted snow. No longer hungry and thirsty, they made beds of leaves and moss. And that night they were able to get their first full night's sleep in almost two weeks.

CHAPTER 5

Three Reach Safety

During their first night on South Georgia, more heavy weather damaged the *Caird*. The little boat was almost lost to the sea. Shackleton had to reach the whaling station on the other side of the island. He knew that in order to do so he was going to have to walk the twenty-mile distance over glaciers and ice-covered mountains. It had never been done before.

He was determined to try to cross on foot. And he knew that it would take all of his skill and bravery. If he tried sailing the *Caird* around the island to the station, chances were that it would be crushed against the rocks and destroyed. This meant that the men on Elephant Island would probably starve to death by the time help arrived.

When the weather cleared, Shackleton, Worsley, and the only other member of the crew who was fit to travel, Crean, prepared for the long hike. They would have to leave the other two behind.

They set off with fifty feet of rope, a two-day supply of food, and a single carpenter's ax. Worsley guided them with a compass. Roping themselves together, so that they would not get separated, the three men found themselves lost in blind passes. Once, by mistake, they made their way back to the sea and had to turn around again.

They hiked to the top of a very steep slope. A sea fog was rolling in behind them, and darkness was falling ahead of them. They had reached a point of no return. They could not go back. But neither could they stay there. If a gale blew in, they would freeze to death. And cutting steps

down the side of the icy mountain slope would be much too slow. They couldn't last.

Even though it was a risk, Shackleton told the others that the three of them would have to slide down the mountain. They had no idea how steep it really was. Darkness had now settled upon them.

They cut out one step in the ice with the ax. Then they wound the rope around them, locking themselves together tightly. Shackleton, in the lead, kicked off. For a moment, the three men seemed to shoot out into space. After the first shock, they actually began to enjoy the slide down the side of the dangerous slope. Racing at nearly sixty miles an hour, they found themselves laughing and yelling loudly. As they slowed down and reached the bottom, they crashed into a soft snowbank. No one had been hurt. What had started out as a hopeless task had turned out to be fun!

They picked themselves up out of the snow-bank, shook hands, and congratulated one another on their success. They moved away from the ridge before they shared a well-earned dinner. They were afraid that the warmth of their campfire might start an avalanche.

After their short meal, the little band set out again. This time they moved up a gentle slope that led to the edge of a snowfield. The moon shown down brightly upon it. Bone-weary, but close to their destination, Shackleton allowed Worsley and Crean to sleep for five minutes. Then he woke them, telling them that they had had almost an hour's rest.

The three made their way through a jagged line of peaks. Ahead of them they saw a welcome sight—Husvik Harbor. Now they were sure that they were finally on the right track. They faced the last twelve miles of difficult country that still lay before them with fresh spirit.

Shackleton left Worsley and Crean behind to prepare breakfast. He went ahead to see what he could see. Suddenly, he stopped in his tracks. His ears perked up. Could it be?

Faintly, from a distance, he thought he could hear the sound of a steam whistle. Civilization at last! The hope was nearly too great. A whistle could mean that they were nearing the whaling station.

Shackleton eagerly took out his watch and looked at the time. It was 7:00 A.M. Exactly the time that a steam whistle would be blowing at the whaling station, calling the men to work. It sounded again, music to his ears.

He hurried back to his companions with the news. They quickly ate their small breakfast and set out again. But there were still many dangers to pass before they would reach the safety of the whaling station. They made their way down the steep slopes. Once they almost sank into a hidden lake buried beneath a crust of snow. At last, they rounded a ridge and caught sight of Stromness Bay, the location of the station.

A small steamer was entering the bay. The masts of a large sailing ship could be seen in the wharf. Most cheering of all was the sight of tiny figures on their way to a large factory, going about their daily business. They had made it!

They made their way down one last mountainside and lowered each other through a waterfall. It was their last obstacle. The way now lay clearly ahead toward safety for them and rescue for the men on the other side of the island,

as well as those left behind on Elephant Island.

Shackleton, Worsley, and Crean took stock of themselves. They knew that they did not present a very pretty picture. Still, they approached the whaling station. They were not surprised when two little boys ran from them, frightened at the sight of the worn-out, filthy men.

Everyone at the station knew who Shackleton was. They had heard about his being lost in the ice along with the rest of the crew of the *Endurance*. However, he was not immediately recognized when he and his comrades entered the office of the whaling station's manager that day. But when they explained who they were, word spread quickly throughout the station. A crowd gathered.

CHAPTER 6

They Were All There!

Shackleton was anxious for news of the war in Europe. But he was first interested in getting some food, hot water to wash in, and fresh clothes. Most of all, though, he was in a rush to form a party to return first to the other side of the island and then to Elephant Island to rescue the men who were counting on him.

That night, as Worsley and Crean slept soundly and warmly in their beds, a good dinner in their stomachs, Shackleton could get no rest. He prayed that he would be able to get the rest of the men of the expedition to safety—and soon.

He stayed behind while Worsley and Crean boarded a whaler to take them around the island to the two men who had been left under the lifeboat there. At first, the two survivors did not recognize Worsley. Now that he was washed and shaved, they thought he was one of the Norwegians who worked at the whaling station. When they realized who it really was, they had a joyous reunion. The whaler sailed at full speed back to the station.

Shackleton, meanwhile, was readying a small whaler, called the *Southern Sky*. It was to make the trip back to Elephant Island. For the next hundred days, he, Worsley, and Crean were to fight the harsh weather, and many other natural obstacles as they tried to get to the men who had been left on the island.

Shackleton had been warned about taking such a small craft back into the dreaded ice pack. But the safety of the men on Elephant Island was first in his mind. He thought it was the most important mission he would ever have to face.

On the first attempt to reach the island, the *Southern Sky* was able to come within sixty miles of it. But the whaler had to turn back when the ice and snowstorms became too much for it.

Using a sturdier vessel, Shackleton tried again. This time, they got as close as eighteen miles from their destination. The ice again forced them back. A thick fog surrounded the island. Shackleton saw the fog as a blessing. He felt that if any of the men were still alive, they would be spared the sight of the ship so near but yet not able to make it to shore. He could imagine the great disappointment at seeing rescue come so close and then failing.

A third rescue party set out. It too failed. It seemed to Shackleton that he was never going to get his men off Elephant Island. He became more and more depressed. Shackleton felt that he had betrayed the trust that these loyal men had placed in him.

The government of Chile lent him a small steamer named the *Yelcho* for his fourth attempt. This time, they became lost in the fog themselves. They could not spot the island. Suddenly, the fog began to clear, and Shackleton saw the

upturned lifeboat that the men had been using as their shelter.

He raised his binoculars to his eyes to count the tiny figures he saw emerging from the makeshift hut on shore when they spotted the little *Yelcho*. Anxiously, he began counting them. Then he let out a cry of joy. They were all there! They had survived!

After a happy reunion aboard the steamer, the survivors told Shackleton that they knew all along that The Boss would not let them down.

To keep up their spirits, each morning every man rolled up his bag and prepared himself for the rescue that they knew was at hand. They had never given up hope. Hearing this cheered Shackleton almost as much as the actual rescue of the men. He had not let them down. Even though he had had many doubts about himself and his abilities, he had never once lost the confidence of his men.

The entire team returned to civilization after their long suffering. When they returned to their homes, most of the men joined the fighting forces to help defend their country. Some of them lost their lives in the war. But none of them ever again had to live through anything as frightening as what had happened to them in Antarctica.

Sadly, Sir Ernest Shackleton was never able to make good his dream of crossing Antarctica on foot. Six months after taking the men off Elephant Island, he died.

Of all his explorations and achievements, it is strange that Shackleton's greatest victory came out of a journey that failed. But it proves that a person's spirit and the will to live can last longer than the short moment of public cheers and fame.

Shackleton had turned near tragedy into a shining victory.